Original title:
Grapefruit Skies

Copyright © 2025 Creative Arts Management OÜ
All rights reserved.

Author: Benjamin Caldwell
ISBN HARDBACK: 978-1-80586-471-4
ISBN PAPERBACK: 978-1-80586-943-6

Skyward Citrus Reflections

A fruit parade up high, so zesty,
Plump oranges bouncing, feeling testy.
Lemons giggle as they spin around,
Juicy laughter echoes, a silly sound.

Clouds in tangerine, they dance with glee,
Waltzing sprites on a fruity spree.
Pulp-based jokes, ripe with delight,
Twinkling compotes under the light.

Radiance of Fruitful Hours

Citrus giggles in the golden sun,
Lemonade rivers, let's have some fun!
Sunsets burst like soda pop,
Squeezy moments that never stop.

Bouncing beams on a playful breeze,
Tasting sunshine with every tease.
A laughter fest, cheeky and bright,
Fruits in a frenzy, what a sight!

Ethereal Sunset Glow

Peachy beams stretch across the sky,
Cotton candy clouds that wave bye-bye.
In the twilight, flavors unite,
Zesty dreams take flight each night.

Spritz of laughter, sprinkle of cheer,
Citrus colors, they're all here!
A fruit fiesta, wild and free,
Watch the world in fruity jubilee.

Melodies of Orange and Pink

Harmonies twirl in a sunset whirl,
Cotton candy fluffs begin to unfurl.
Giggling grapefruits play hide and seek,
Ticklish tones in a fruity peak.

Chasing tangerines through the day,
Fuzzy feelings that won't decay.
As colors blend, the fun won't quit,
Joyful juiciness, every little bit.

The Sweetness of Twilit Hues

In twilight's glow, the fruit does sway,
With zest for life, they hide away.
A yellow orb with a wink so sly,
Makes sour faces laugh and pry.

A bite so bold, it makes you sing,
Pulp confessions and zestful fling.
Rolling laughter, seeds take flight,
As juicy jokes fill up the night.

Vermilion Echoes

When the sun dips low, colors burst,
Citrus giggles in a fruity thirst.
Orange hues with a cheeky grin,
Squeeze the day out, let the fun begin.

Lemonades past, high-sour dreams,
Dance with cheers and spritely schemes.
Beneath the clouds, the flavors clash,
A zesty laugh, a blush, a splash.

Dusk's Citrus Invitation

Dusk plays coy, the colors blend,
With a wink and zest, they extend.
Tart little elves bounce on the breeze,
Tickling senses just to tease.

Oranges whisper silly tales,
As laughter drifts and never fails.
Here's to secrets in the twilight,
Where zesty joy takes flight at night.

Juicy Echoes of Solitude

In quiet moments, citrus bright,
Playful echoes tease the night.
Sour sprites hide in the peel,
Telling tales that make you squeal.

Pondering life in fruity plots,
Tickled by giggles in sunny spots.
A slice of humor, a wink so bold,
Juicy secrets waiting to unfold.

Pastel Dreams Above

Cotton candy clouds float high,
Bouncing with laughter from the sky.
A lemon slice moon, grinning wide,
Winks at the stars as they slide.

Silly birds in shades of pink,
Chirp tunes that make the sun rethink.
Dancing sunbeams, twirl around,
Painting the world with joy unbound.

Sunset Serenade in Vermilion

The sun bows low with a silly grin,
Kicking off shoes, ready to spin.
Blushing oranges dip in the sea,
Tickling waves with giggles of glee.

A flamingo serenades the dusk,
In vibrant hues, it's a must.
Sassy shadows in a playful race,
Chasing each other, keeping pace.

Zesty Shimmers of Twilight

Twilight sneezes, a burst of zest,
The sky erupts in laughter, a jest.
Juggling stars that giggle and twirl,
With a wink, they make the night whirl.

Lemon drops from heavens so bright,
Scatter sugar on the velvet night.
Oranges chuckle, while tarts play coy,
In the zesty ballet, there's much joy.

Heavenly Citrus Canvas

A canvas painted with fruity cheer,
Where colors dance without any fear.
Citrus giggles ripple through the air,
While sunsets chuckle without a care.

Breezy whispers tickle the trees,
As laughter mingles with the breeze.
Each splash of color sings a tune,
Making mischief with the happy moon.

Tinge of Sunset's Bite

A fruit so bright, it pouts in glee,
Their zesty smiles, a fruity spree.
Each slice bursts forth, a sunset cheer,
With every bite, who needs a beer?

Juicy orbs in a swirl of gold,
They laugh and dance, they won't be told.
On picnic blankets, they make their stand,
Squeezing sunshine from every hand.

Eclipsed in Citrus Light

Under a lamp, it shines so bold,
Its laughter echoes, sweet and cold.
Chasing shadows with a wink and grin,
This citrus star where fun begins.

When life gets dull, and skies are gray,
A dash of zest will save the day.
With every twist, it giggles loud,
It's the citrus king, so bright and proud.

Sunset in a Bottle

In jars it swirls, a sunset blend,
Tart and sweet, a flavor friend.
Pop the cork, let laughter flow,
This bottled joy steals every show.

Pour it out and watch it fizz,
Giggles bubble, oh what a whiz!
Each sip a chuckle, a taste delight,
A party in a glass, so free and bright.

Resplendent Citrus Veils

With peels like laughter in the breeze,
Each wedge a joke that aims to please.
They jest and play on kitchen shelves,
In sunny light, they tease themselves.

With every squeeze, a dance of zest,
They're the jester in the fruit fest.
Wrapped in colors, vibrant and spry,
Citrus fun beneath the sky.

Coral Clouds Above

The clouds are pink like candy floss,
Lollipop dreams in a citrus gloss.
Birds wearing shades fly in a daze,
Looking for snacks in the sunlit haze.

A squirrel dressed up, he's ready to dance,
While a cat on a roof gives a side-eye glance.
All the colors wave and sway,
In a world that's quirky, come what may.

Citrus Sunsets

Orange peels flicker, the night wears a grin,
As crickets croon songs, let the laughter begin.
The moon's made of cheese, or maybe a slice,
As llamas in sunglasses roll dice in paradise.

Stars throw confetti; the night's a grand ball,
With giggles of clouds as they tumble and sprawl.
Each breeze brings a chuckle, soft whispers so fun,
Under citrus sunsets, we dance until done.

Twilight's Tangy Kiss

Twilight drizzles with a splash of delight,
Where pickles hang out, and laugh until night.
A jester in pie shoes spins round with a flair,
As kumquats giggle from their comfy chair.

Socks on the line start a tango so sweet,
While lemons play tag on the warm, grassy seat.
With each tangy wink, the day drips away,
In twilight's embrace, we all want to stay.

Juicy Dreams at Dusk

Dusk rolls in with a splash and a pop,
Grapes in their jammies start a rooftop hop.
A pickle parade in the moon's mellow light,
With carrots and celery, all giggles in sight.

The stars are jiggling; it's quite the buffet,
While cucumbers moonwalk and salsa, hooray!
In juicy dreams where the fruit bowls burst,
Laughter is plenty, and joy is rehearsed.

Orange Blossom Dreams at Sundown

In the garden of whimsy, I find my glee,
Where the sun winks at clouds as they dance with me.
Petals twirl in the breeze, oh what a sight,
A jester's cap made of citrus delight.

Lemons giggle as oranges roll by,
In a fruit parade under a sunset sky.
With every sip of laughter, the world seems bright,
I toast with a slice to this fruity delight.

Twilight's Zesty Cascade

The sun sets with a crunch, like a snack on the run,
A splash of zest in the air, oh, what fun!
Laughter pours out as the stars take their place,
With tangerine dreams racing all over the space.

Jokes land like fruit drops, sweet and absurd,
As the night unfolds, swirl and twirl, unheard.
The sky turns punchy, a fizzy delight,
We sip on the giggles 'til stars smile bright.

Taste of Twilight's Eden

In twilight's embrace, flavor tickles the tongue,
With chuckles and cheers, our adventure is young.
The moon dons a smile, lemons gleam with cheer,
Each sip of our joy makes the twilight more dear.

We juggle the moments, they bounce and they play,
Like fruit on a splash mat, bright and okay.
The night's full of flavors, tangy and sweet,
In our Eden of laughter, life's truly a treat.

Sun-Washed Hues and Hazy Promises

The sky paints a canvas, all sticky and bright,
Hazy promises linger, both sour and light.
With brushes of laughter, I'm whirling with glee,
As I bump into oranges that giggle at me.

Sun-washed and wobbly, the world does a jig,
Every step is a dance, oh you ought to take a swig!
In this zany sunset, life's quirkiest wine,
We sip on wild colors, tangy and divine.

Sunset Hues of Citrus Dreams

A wink of orange in the air,
As the day sends off a flair.
Lemons giggle, limes take flight,
Dancing shadows in the night.

Blushing clouds like fruit in bloom,
Chasing boredom to its doom.
Juicy laughter fills the sky,
As cheerful birds just fly by.

Whispers of a Tangerine Dawn

Morning stretches with a smile,
While oranges roll and dance a mile.
Citrus kisses greet the sun,
A tangy start, oh what a fun!

Squirrels sip on juicy dew,
As laughter echoes, bright and new.
Oh, what mischief, what a scene,
In this world of tangerine!

Blushing Oranges in Twilight

Twilight blushes, time to play,
With citrus charms that light the way.
Bananas laugh, so silly, sweet,
As night takes on a fruity beat.

Stars sprinkle zest across the dark,
While fruit delights make their mark.
Even shadows wear a grin,
In this world, we spin and spin!

A Canvas of Pinks and Peaches

Brushstrokes of pink, a peachy hue,
Art supplies shaped like fruit, it's true.
When laughter spills, and colors blend,
A fruity twist, the fun won't end.

Palette of giggles, spread it wide,
With funky flavors as our guide.
Swinging high on citrus dreams,
Life's a joke, or so it seems!

Cosmic Citrus Reverie

In a land where the fruit flies,
Juggling stars and pies,
A banana wearing shades,
Laughs at the sun's bright raids.

Lemons on tightropes sway,
Chasing each other's rays,
An orange tells a joke,
While peaches giggle and choke.

Over the Horizon of Melon Clouds

Bouncing high on melon boats,
Watermelon caps and coats,
A crew of zesty zest,
Hoping for a juicy quest.

They sail on waves of juice,
With tangerines as the moose,
Chewing gum on the mast,
Hoping the fun will last.

Juicy Reflections at Dusk

The sun drips like an orange slice,
While limes roll and entice,
A grapefruit dreams afloat,
In a boat made of toast.

At dusk, the colors play,
In a citrus ballet,
Bananas wear tiny hats,
As laughing critters chat.

The Citrus Symphony of Evening

At dusk, the citrics hum,
With a beat that makes you strum,
Kumquats dance on piano keys,
While tangy breezes tease.

The night is sweet and bright,
As grapefruits take flight,
Squeezing melodies from the stars,
In their fruity, shining cars.

Peachy Clouds of Tomorrow's Light

Fluffy pink wonders float so high,
Above the laughter, as kites do fly.
Bouncing dreams on sugary beams,
Tickled by sunlight, or so it seems.

Chasing giggles on soft, sweet winds,
Where silly hats and joy begins.
Wobbly struts on candy-coated clouds,
Making the cosmos erupt in crowds.

Radiance of Citrus Kisses

Sunshine wrapped in a zesty bow,
Like silly faces, vibrant and slow.
Lemon drops tumble, tickling toes,
As everyone dances and joyfully glows.

Squeezy hugs from orange days,
Bright wit sparkles in cheerful rays.
Laughter zips like a bright parade,
As frothy drinks in hand are made.

Both Sweet and Tangy Evenings

Bubbling laughs on a tangerine breeze,
As stars play peek-a-boo between the trees.
Fizzy jokes in the dusky air,
Graze the night with a citrus flair.

Wobble and giggle with sticky fingers,
While the funny taste of twilight lingers.
Zesty malarkey fills the dreamy sky,
With each silly grin, our spirits fly.

Breathe in the Zesty Air

Whimsical wisps of citrus delight,
Whirling and twirling through shimmering light.
Silly thoughts drift like candy canes,
Carrying laughter through vibrant lanes.

Giggling breezes, a fruity parade,
Where mischievous fun is never delayed.
Each breath a burst of ticklish cheer,
In a world where smiles are always near.

Citrus Dreams in the Ether

In the land of fruit and quirk,
Chasing zest as colors lurk.
Orange clouds with giggles gleam,
Juicy laughter fills the dream.

Lemon slices pave the way,
Dancing echo of the play.
Twists and turns like citrus swirls,
As ridiculous as it twirls.

Banana peels fly overhead,
Tropical tunes that must be said.
Bubblegum clouds with a squeeze,
Ticklish breezes, oh what tease!

Each sunset peels a new delight,
Silly shadows take to flight.
In this world all things are bright,
We revel in the citrus light.

Candied Skies at Dusk

Sugary hues paint the air,
Cotton candy, laughter rare.
Popcorn puffs dot the horizon,
Curious dreams like frizzled bison.

Bubblegum kisses on the breeze,
Lemonade rivers tease with ease.
Lollipop stars burst overhead,
Nonsense fills each word that's said.

Jellybean's having a ball,
Underneath the gumdrop hall.
Dancing in sugary delight,
Silly twirls through the night.

Every gust brings a chuckle here,
As candy-coated clouds appear.
With each puff, we prance and sway,
In this sweet sky, we'll forever play.

The Citron Dreams We Hold

Citron wishes on a fling,
Bouncing bright on laughter's wing.
Pineapple friends join the show,
Jesting under the citrus glow.

Tickling clouds of tangy joy,
Here we giggle, girl and boy.
With each squirt, surprises wait,
Tickled by the whims of fate.

Sour twists and sweetened sighs,
As jazzy fruit composes lies.
Every shade a funny tale,
In this world where we set sail.

Together in zesty cheer,
We toast to dreams that bring us near.
In the citrus-themed delight,
Laughter blooms, oh what a sight!

Twilight's Tangy Brushes

Twilight paints with a bouncy brush,
Colors clash in a fruity rush.
Orange giggles fill the scene,
As veggies dance in spaces green.

A lemon drops an offbeat beat,
While carrots shimmies, oh so sweet.
Dancing radishes take the lead,
In this twilight, the fun's our creed.

Starbursts blaze in purple skies,
As broccoli dons a clever disguise.
Frisbee stars that cringe and gleam,
In this realm of silly theme.

So let us feast on laughter bold,
With twilight's tales yet untold.
In this tangy, joking light,
We play beneath the stars so bright.

Sunlit Citrus Tapestry

Orange fluff in a sunny glow,
Bouncing clouds like kids at a show.
Lemon slices skip with glee,
Twirling around like they're fancy and free.

Limes make jokes, they're quite the jest,
Poking fun at the sour, no time to rest.
A tangerine giggles, what a wild ride,
Chasing the sunlight, it's a zestful slide.

Under the sun, they dance and prance,
In their fruity costumes, they take a chance.
Peeling laughter fills the air,
In this citrus world, nothing else compares.

The Twilight Blend

As the day winks with a wink so sly,
Juicy mocktails wave goodbye.
Poppy oranges blending with red,
Joking around, while lounging in bed.

Twilight chuckles, dreams float high,
Lemon drops giggling, oh my, oh my!
A sip of laughter in every glass,
Sipping fun as the moments pass.

Strawberries hum a silly tune,
Dancing stars above like balloons.
With each sparkle, they share a laugh,
Twilight's humor, a bubbly craft.

Pinks and Peels of Dusk

Peeling colors in the fading light,
A berry brigade ready for flight.
Crimson giggles tickle the trees,
As laughter rustles through the leaves.

Citrus critters play hide and seek,
Chasing the sun with a cheeky squeak.
Pastel hues make playful pranks,
Blushing the sky with their happy ranks.

With every squeeze, their joy will spill,
A fruity circus dancing on the hill.
As dusk giggles and hugs the day,
The colors swirl, in a frolicsome play.

The Glow of Day's Goodbye

As the sun takes its final bow,
Fruits whisper secrets, "wow, oh wow!"
Orange giggles stretch across the land,
Fruits unite, all hand in hand.

The day departs with a bright, loud cheer,
Leaving behind joy for all to hear.
Ruby reds sparkle with a laugh,
In the twilight glow, they share a gaffe.

A bubbly farewell, so sweet and sly,
As peaches wink and lemons sigh.
In this playful scene, they twirl and glide,
At the close of day, joy won't hide.

Sunkissed Mood

With laughter bright and breezy air,
The sun's a jester, full of flair.
It dances on our carefree heads,
In golden rays, our worries shed.

The fruit of fun just starts to show,
Like sticky juice, we laugh and glow.
Beneath the warmth, we skip and play,
A silly chase 'til end of day.

With cheeks all flushed and spirits high,
We're fruity treasure, you and I.
A burst of joy, a zesty swirl,
In this wild, sun-drenched world.

Palette of the Senses

What's this hue, a playful sight?
A palette painted with delight.
With every shade, a giggle forms,
As laughter rises with the storms.

Orange peels and pink delight,
A never-ending comic flight.
Each color sparkles, makes us grin,
Like quirky jokes we weave within.

The brush of life is wild and free,
As jokes collide, just you and me.
A canvas stretched, chance to explore,
In vivid tones, we laugh for more.

Pinks and Oranges Collide

When pinks and oranges start to dance,
In quirky twirls, they take a chance.
A clumsy laugh, a playful sway,
They tumble down, in bright array.

A citrus giggle fills the air,
As fruit spills juice without a care.
A splash of color, a splash of fun,
In a fruit salad under the sun.

From silly faces to fruity cheers,
We toast with laughter, forget our fears.
As glowing light begins to fade,
Our funny tales in hues displayed.

Saffron Hues at Twilight

With saffron blush upon the night,
We chase the shadows, what a sight!
As twilight giggles, soft and low,
In dreamy colors, we'll bestow.

Fireflies wink, a playful game,
In this silly, glowing frame.
We'll dance with stars, like clowns on beams,
And spin our hopes in frothy dreams.

The moon can't help but join our fun,
As laughter sparkles, on the run.
In saffron hues, we find our bliss,
With every giggle, that perfect kiss.

Radiant Hues at Sunset

Orange blush upon the trees,
With lemons laughing in the breeze.
The clouds are painting quite a scene,
Like fruit salad, fresh and green.

Silly birds in joyful flight,
Chasing shadows, pure delight.
They think the sun is one big snack,
But watch it vanish, sneak attack!

Bouncing light, a circus act,
As nature pulls its magic tact.
The world begins to play pretend,
In colors that just never end.

So as the sun dips out of sight,
We giggle at this foodie fight.
With fruity dreams, we wave goodnight,
Until the stars join in the light.

Alchemy of Dusk

When day turns into tasty dusk,
We ponder colors, sweet and brusque.
A blend of flavors, up so high,
As whispers of the night pass by.

The sun dips low, a golden treat,
While clouds bloom like a sugary feat.
Who knew the sky could look so bold,
Like candy wrappers, bright and gold?

Fireflies dance, they wear their glow,
As twilight sings its silly show.
A potion mix of shade and light,
In every corner, pure delight.

As laughter echoes, softly spreads,
We fill the night with half-baked threads.
And in this magic, oh so vast,
We hope this funny spell will last.

Vermillion Embrace of Night

A twilight wrap of bright vermilion,
The stars descend in soft rebellion.
Shadows sidle, wearing grins,
As mischief in the dark begins.

Laughter spills from every tree,
As nighttime plays its tricks with glee.
The moon, a cheeky little chap,
Peeks out from clouds as if to nap.

With giggles hidden, soft and sweet,
The night unveils its fruity beat.
A sassy breeze that tickles toes,
While midnight blooms in silly clothes.

Oh evening, give your fruit parade,
With crimson shades, upon us laid.
Each wink of light, a chuckle shared,
In this embrace, we're fully paired.

Citrus Symphony

A zesty tune in evening's heart,
Where oranges and limes take part.
The sky, a canvas so divine,
With melodies of sunlit wine.

A chorus of the laughing stars,
Composing symphonies from Mars.
With every note, a citrus cheer,
As fruity jokes are drawn so near.

Beneath the arch of citrus fair,
We sway and dance without a care.
As light and laughter blend in rhyme,
The night unfolds, a merry time.

So let the rhythm make us sway,
In this fruity ballet, we play.
With sticky fingers, joy ignites,
In this sweet world of silly nights.

Evening's Fruity Farewell

The sun dips low, a citrus glow,
With hues that make the world feel slow.
A squirrel in shades of orange burns,
Gnashing teeth at the day's sweet turns.

Clouds fluff like marshmallows in the mist,
As birds take flight with a fruity twist.
They squawk and chirp, a raucous cheer,
For the day's end, they hold so dear.

The breeze is tangy, a light caress,
Tickling my nose with fruitiness.
I laugh aloud at the colors bright,
As laughter dances in the dying light.

In twilight's laughter, we give a toast,
To the flavors that we love the most.
With eyes aglow, we bid adieu,
To the evening dressed in zestful hue.

Dusk's Zesty Lullaby

In the fading light, a citrus tune,
Chirps of crickets serenade the moon.
Lemonade thoughts swirl in the breeze,
As laughter spills like honeyed tease.

Orange halos around the trees,
The playful wind tickles with ease.
A dancing cat with a playful leap,
Winks at the sky, then drifts to sleep.

Polka-dot clouds parade on high,
As fireflies twinkle, an evening pie.
With every flicker, the night's delight,
Tickles my heart like grapefruit bite.

The stars join in with a giggling glow,
As the world wraps up in a zesty row.
With chuckles woven into the night,
Dusk drapes us all in fruity light.

Flavors of the Setting Sun

As day rolls out in a cotton candy swirl,
The sky puts on its peachy twirl.
Giggling clouds in a fruity spree,
Play peek-a-boo with the bumblebee.

The sun winks down with a fruity jest,
Painting the horizon in a colorful fest.
Jellybean laughter rises so sweet,
As evening stoplights flash and greet.

A parade of colors, each more absurd,
Tickling my senses without a word.
With every hue, a chuckle burst,
In this silly ranch we call the earth.

So let the sun set with all its flair,
As we giggle on, without a care.
For every dusk brings joy anew,
In flavors bold, and giggles too.

The Lush Horizon of Evening

In the twilight's fruity glow,
Squirrels dance with zestful flow.
They juggle seeds and tell tall tales,
As laughter flies on evening gales.

Funky fruit flies buzz about,
In this world, there's never doubt.
Each orange slice, a smile to share,
As birds chirp jokes hanging in air.

The clouds are painted tart and sweet,
Where monkeys tap their tiny feet.
They swing on hues of fog and cheer,
With snappy quips that tickle ear.

A fruit fiesta in the dusk,
Balloons of juice go pop with fuss.
The stars join in, a zesty choir,
In this funny twilight fire.

Reflections in Sunset's Orchard

Beneath the trees where rabbits peek,
Chasing shadows with a squeak.
Dancing leaves, a silly breeze,
Twists and turns with such a tease.

A raccoon wears a fruit hat proud,
Singing karaoke, drawing a crowd.
Each note a slice of joy unspooled,
As creatures laugh, the night is fueled.

In the orchard ripe with chuckles,
A pear drops down and softly snuggles.
The humor's thick, the shadows play,
As laughter peeks in golden spray.

Fireflies blink like winking pies,
While frogs recite their silly lies.
In this patch of twilight'sweet,
Life feels like fruit, all fun and neat.

Citrus Horizon

On the edge of dusk, a zesty grin,
Where lemons twirl and oranges spin.
A piñata party in the trees,
As laughter bounces on the breeze.

Toucan wears a party hat,
While gophers share their garden spat.
A game of limbo under the sun,
With every pass, more laughs begun.

The scent of citrus fills the air,
Frogs line up for a daring dare.
Jump in line, they hop and weave,
All in fun, they never leave.

In this silly place up high,
Jokes fly like low-flying pie.
With every twist and every turn,
In sunset's glow, we laugh and learn.

Evening's Blush

Underneath the blush of night,
Silly shadows take to flight.
Chickens dance in pastel glow,
As laughter echoes, stealing show.

A cat in boots, a wise old sage,
Tells tales of fruits upon a stage.
Each rhyme a slice, each joke a cheer,
As giggles ripple, warm and clear.

The moon joins in with a cheeky wink,
Spinning fables, push and brink.
A jam session with crickets inside,
Spinning tunes on evening's tide.

As stars fall down like jelly beans,
To light the night with silly scenes.
In evening's blush, fun takes its flight,
Banishing calm, igniting delight.

Sunset Splash of Citrus

A fruit bowl spins in evening light,
Lemons wearing shades, what a sight!
Oranges dance with a zestful grin,
While limes pretend they're cool within.

The sunset drips like a juice connoisseur,
Squeezing out giggles, that is for sure!
Citrus clouds puff in a silly parade,
As laughter bursts like a lemon-flavored grenade.

Bananas slip in the tangy show,
Their peels like slippers, oh what a blow!
Pineapples cheer with a crown on high,
In this silly land, where all fruits fly!

As day packs up its citrus punch,
They all sit down to a fruity brunch!
Bubbly drinks made of tangy dreams,
In a world where humor shines and beams.

Radiant Afternoon Light

On a lemon lounge chair, bees debate,
Whether this nectar can truly be great!
Ladybugs giggle at the sun's high peek,
While ants in tuxedos do their routine tweak.

The sun hangs low, a tangerine ball,
Winking at apples having a brawl.
Everyone's ready for a juicy game,
In this crazy world, they're all the same!

Rainbows slide down like slippery juice,
While oranges bounce in a fruity truce.
A dance-off between fruits begins with flair,
As everyone joins, with zest in the air!

Laughter erupts like a fizzy drink,
While grapes twirl 'round, making you think!
This radiant afternoon, so full of cheer,
Is a fruity fiesta we all hold dear.

Tangerine Whispers of Dawn

As dawn breaks open, a tangerine glow,
The world wakes up, feeling quite the show!
Mandarins whisper secrets so sweet,
While apples gossip, 'Look at that treat!'

Sunbeams tickle the curls of the trees,
While pears do a jig and sway in the breeze.
They sip on sunshine with a fruity twist,
Creating a morning no one could miss!

The clouds wear hats of cotton candy fluff,
Bananas remind us to never play tough.
Strawberries burst with a giggly cheer,
They all sing together, "The day is here!"

With laughter aplenty and smiles in play,
Every fruit savors the start of the day,
In a world where joy dances and prances,
Each citrus heart takes funny chances.

Celestial Citrus Glow

Stars twinkle bright with a zesty glow,
Lemons make wishes, and off they go!
Mangoes are astronauts, flying so high,
While cherries giggle as they drift by.

Galaxies swirl in a fizzy delight,
Watermelons rocket through the night.
Peaches wear helmets made of sweet cream,
In this cosmic dance where fruits dare to dream!

The moon, a slice of a juicy peach pie,
Winks at the fruits as they zoom and fly.
Citrus comets dash with a splash,
In this humor-filled night, they make a brash!

As the stars burst in a burst of cheer,
Each fruit shouts, "We have nothing to fear!"
In this celestial realm where happiness ranks,
They twirl together, giving thanks and pranks!

Dawn's Juicy Embrace

The sun bursts forth with a zesty grin,
Bouncing off rooftops, where mischief begins.
Birds chirp in laughter, such a silly sound,
Morning giggles spark joy all around.

A baker drops doughnuts, they roll down the street,
Chasing after squirrels with nimble little feet.
Lemonade stand spills, it's a sticky parade,
Watch out for the sugar rush, sweet escapade!

Waking up yawning with eyes half-closed,
Stumbling on flip-flops, oh, what a pose!
Coffee pot's bubbling, it's bouncing with cheer,
A mug full of giggles, oh dear, oh dear!

Dawn stretches wide in a citrusy pose,
Juggling bright fruit with a bag of old clothes.
With a wink and a laugh, the day pulls in tight,
So let's dance with the sunrise, it feels just right!

Warm Citrus Awakening

Bumbling bees buzz in a lopsided line,
Wiggling their bodies, oh what a design!
Pineapple hats and orange-shaped shoes,
Join the parade of the fruit-loving blues.

Chickens lay eggs that are sunny-side bright,
Clucking their tunes, they're a comical sight.
The baker's doughnuts, a chocolate delight,
Rolling down hills with all of their might!

Oven mitts dancing on toes of the chef,
Spilling hot muffins, oh goodness, what heft!
Juicy juice glasses all clink in a cheer,
Sipping and slipping, oh dear, oh dear!

A seamstress is threading bright ribbons of sun,
Stitching up laughter – oh, this is such fun!
Soft clouds all giggle, tickling the sea,
A warm citrus hug, come laugh along with me!

Sweetness in the Sky

Clouds fluffy like marshmallows float in delight,
Cotton candy dreams making everything bright.
Sunshine sprinkles laughter like it's confetti,
A sweet, silly whirlwind, all of us ready!

Balloons bobbing high, like they're dancing around,
Each twist and turn brings giggles profound.
Float like a jellybean, twirl with a grin,
A carnival of joy where fun must begin!

Neighbors trade jokes in a citrusy haze,
Laughter just echoes, oh, what a phase!
Sippin' on smoothies, we toast to the sun,
Melodies of happiness - oh, what fun!

With laughter like sugar, let's swirl through the air,
Dance with the wind and not a single care.
Underneath pink streaks where the sun likes to play,
A sweet little world, come join in today!

Melon Flames of Evening

As day waves goodbye with its peach-colored flair,
Watermelon wishes float high in the air.
The stars peek out with a mischievous grin,
Silly shadows dance on the cheek of a spin.

Grilled veggies center stage, making all the calls,
Chillin' with salsa at evening's bright balls.
Giggles on blankets like candy we share,
Laughter resounding is felt everywhere!

Ice-cream cones wobble atop little hands,
Everyone's bouncing in colorful bands.
Fireflies winking as daylight takes flight,
Evening ignites with a playful delight!

Underneath stars like sprinkles, we bask,
With beat of our hearts, join the nighttime task.
Melon flames dance in the night's cozy glow,
Endless fun with friends, let the laughter flow!

Golden Zest between the Stars

Underneath the quirky moon,
The fruit parade begins its tune.
Tangled laughs in citrus dreams,
Where nothing's quite as it seems.

The night, a canvas of bright cheer,
Where even clouds wear smiles near.
We juggle laughter, toss our glee,
As stars wink back, so playfully.

In fields of whimsy, joy takes flight,
With zestful whispers in the night.
A playful dance of citrus zest,
Invites us all to join the fest.

So come, dear friends, let's spin awhile,
Among the fruit with gleaming style.
For in this world of vibrant fun,
The laughter ripples, never done.

Sunset Glow in Fruity Palette

A splash of orange on the breeze,
Tickles the day, oh, how it teases!
Mango clouds with strawberry hue,
We giggle as the colors skew.

Banana boats on creamy waves,
Sailing to shores where humor braves.
Cantaloupe smiles, radiant and round,
In this sweet dusk, joy is found.

Pineapple sunbeams dance and prance,
While tangy breezes start to glance.
We toast to sunsets, loud and bright,
In fruity fun, our hearts take flight.

So join the ride on zesty streams,
Where playful moments fill our dreams.
In every laugh, in every gleam,
The palette shines, a vivid theme.

The Coral Hour of Day's Embrace

Coral whispers to the day,
As waves of laughter come to play.
Citrus giggles in the breeze,
The sun agrees, it's time to tease.

Lavender dreams on candied skies,
With footprints made of sweet surprise.
Raspberry clouds, so softly spun,
Invite us all to laugh and run.

Fruity fables twirl and sway,
In this whimsical ballet.
With every giggle, joy unfolds,
As coral hues break out in golds.

So gather 'round, let's share a cheer,
On this bright avenue of cheer.
For as the day begins to close,
Our funny tales in sunlight pose.

Nectarine Wishes on High

Wishes splash like juicy rain,
Floating dreams that tease the brain.
Nectarine giggles in the air,
Laughter ripe, with fruity flair.

Clouds of caramel swirl and spin,
In the dance of joy, we all win.
Bubblegum whispers in the breeze,
Tickling our hearts with effortless ease.

Peach-faced dreams in twilight glow,
Chasing shadows, off we go!
In the garden of silly dreams,
Life's a joke, or so it seems.

So let the night be bright and sweet,
With zesty giggles, oh so neat.
For nectarines on high remind,
Of laughter shared and joy enshrined.

A Flush of Color on the Edge of Night

When the sun slips on a banana peel,
And the clouds giggle in orange zeal.
The evening pops in a fruity flair,
As light dances without a care.

Pink edges sprout on the horizon wide,
Like candy floss with nowhere to hide.
Jester hues paint the twilight stage,
As night's laughter turns the page.

The Sunkissed Veil of Dusk

Behold the sky in a citrus steer,
Where silly shades swing without fear.
The day bows down, a comedy show,
As the curtain of dusk starts to glow.

A tangerine hat tips to the bright,
While zebras prance in warm twilight.
Whimsical whirls of laughter chase,
In this cerulean, colorful place.

A Burst of Colorful Hopes

In the twilight, crayons play on high,
With scribbles of joy that flutter by.
Hues dance merrily from tree to tree,
Whispering jokes among the bumblebees.

Every hue's a prank waiting to tease,
As oranges wiggle in the activating breeze.
With every burst, there's laughter around,
Colorful hopes on the ground are found.

Melodies of the Early Moon

As the moon pulls up a disco ball,
Stars are guests at a light-hearted ball.
Each twinkle hums a jolly tune,
In funny shades of silvery swoon.

Lunar laughs spill on the grassy floor,
Where fireflies strut and summer's encore.
The night's orchestra tunes up with glee,
As moonbeams giggle, wild and free.

The Lingering Shade of Citrus

In a land where oranges dance,
And lemons wear a funny stance,
Tangerines giggle in the breeze,
While limes craft jokes with utmost ease.

The clouds are fluffy, sweet and bright,
Wearing zestful coats, what a sight!
They tickle each other with silly rhymes,
While the sun is snorting, laughing in chimes.

The trees all sway to an unseen tune,
As the squirrels play hopscotch under the moon,
Their puns are fresh, like a citrus fling,
As the whole grove starts to laugh and sing.

So let the citrus shade be here,
With lemon-laden laughter and cheer,
For in this world of tangy delight,
Life is a joke, oh what a sight!

Dreams Captured in Color

In the garden where colors burst,
Dreams float by, oh, how they thirst,
For a sip of something sweet and bold,
In hues of gold, orange, and cold.

Pink clouds whisper with jellybean laughs,
Chasing fruit-shaped clouds on sunny paths,
They throw confetti, a citrus parade,
While windmills spin in a citrus charade.

The stars wear hats made of candy light,
Tickling dreams into the night,
While juicy dreams chase one another,
In a glorious mess, like sister and brother.

So pluck the sweetness from the sky,
Dance with colors, oh my, oh my,
For in this world, we play and twirl,
In every shade, we'll swirl and whirl!

Celestial Melodies at Dusk

The sun bows down with a citrus grin,
As twilight chuckles, where do we begin?
Dancing dust flutters, like tiny sprites,
While stars are (no kidding!) bundled up tight.

A moon on stilts, wearing puffy shoes,
Whispers secrets to the drowsy blues,
With a banjo strum from a starry band,
The universe croons, it's simply grand!

Lemonade lakes swirl, with ripples of fun,
While cooler fruits melt beneath the sun,
And every laugh echoes through the night,
In the pitch and roll of the cosmic flight.

So find your rhythm in the dusky chill,
Every note and giggle, a sweetness to fill,
As we sway to celestial tunes with glee,
In a funny world, you just wait and see!

Reflections of a Citrus Sunset

At the close of day where limes collide,
Orange glimmers play, oh what a ride,
Each sunset beams with a teasing smirk,
As shadows leap up with a joyful perk.

Reflective waters ripple with cheer,
While clouds flirt round with citrus flair,
Jokesters among the oranges and greens,
In a world where nonsense reigns like queens.

Juicy tales bounce like laughter's spark,
As day dims down, igniting the dark,
With a wink from green in the twilight glow,
Every citrus pun makes the laughter flow.

So gather the beams of this glowing sight,
Let the sunset tickle you good tonight,
For in these reflections, love's never far,
In a juicy world, we're all bizarre!

Alpenglow of Citrus Fragrance

The sun dips low, in a juicy glow,
Painting clouds in orange and yellow.
Bees are buzzing, in a citrus song,
While squirrels dance, all day long.

Lemons roll like marbles, in the grass,
Limes perform the tango, oh so fast.
A fruit parade, on the green hill,
Nature's laughter, gives a thrill.

Citrus peels like confetti rain,
Each zesty whiff, drives me insane.
With every squeeze, a giggle escapes,
Watch out for those slippery grapes!

At twilight's call, all citrus smiles,
Waving goodbye in fruity styles.
The air is sweet, and life feels light,
As day gives way to silly night.

Kissed by the Citrus Light

Waking up to zesty delight,
Morning sun, a citrus height.
Orange hugs the horizon tight,
Coffee's jealous of the sight.

Chasing shadows, in citrus suits,
Dancing in my funny boots.
Grapefruits giggle on the tree,
Life's a joke, come laugh with me!

The wind whispers tales of lime,
As I waltz through this sweet rhyme.
Melons chuckle from afar,
Underneath the vaudeville star.

When evening falls, oh what a treat,
Citrus dreams can't be beat.
Beneath the chuckles, all seems right,
Kissed and twirled, by citrus light.

The Last Sip of Day

As daylight sips its last, I'm told,
That oranges blush, their tales unfold.
Kiwis whisper secrets low,
As twilight paints the world aglow.

With every breeze, a giggle here,
From fruity faces, full of cheer.
The final drop, a punchline bright,
Fruits are frolicking, what a sight!

Every sunset bursts with zest,
Nature's stand-up, at its best.
Lime and lemon, share a grin,
As night begins, let laughter win!

So I sip slow, this fruity cheer,
With citrus puns that draw us near.
The day wraps up, with laughter's sway,
In the last sip of this bright day.

Melon Hues of Reflection

In the quiet pond, melons reflect,
Wiggling fish, playfully connect.
Pink and green, a playful show,
Even the frogs start to glow.

Sunbeams bounce on melon rinds,
Each ripple giggles, nature finds.
Bouncing berries join the frolic,
In this pool of sweet symbolic.

A watermelon dance, silly and bright,
All the critters join the light.
Juicy thoughts swirl in the air,
As nature giggles without a care.

So let's reflect on this fruity cheer,
Join the fun, come gather near!
Life's a feast of colors, oh so grand,
In melon hues, together we stand.

Tangerine Fragments of Time

In the kitchen, we laugh and scheme,
Peeling oranges, a citrus dream,
Juicy drops drip like silly rain,
Each bite bursts with a zesty gain.

Mom claims it keeps her young and spry,
While Dad just winks and lets out a sigh,
A fruit salad party, what a delight,
Even the dog tries to take a bite!

Bursting segments, like a giggle fits,
Sweet and tangy, that's how it sits,
We toast with slices, laughter flows,
Sticky fingers, but nobody knows.

Time slips away, like juice off the skin,
No cares exist in this juicy din,
With every piece, we share a smile,
Let's savor the flavor, let's stay a while.

Dappled Light in Citrus Tones

Sunlight dances through the trees,
Squeezed out laughter floats in the breeze,
Yellow globes hang, cheeky and bright,
A jester's hat in the morning light.

We skip on paths lined with zest,
Bicycle wheels spin like a jester's jest,
Chasing shadows, we search for fun,
Every citrus slice feels like a pun.

The dog prances with a twist of fate,
In pursuit of lemons he'd dare not rate,
Yet when he bites, he jumps and yips,
The prankster ghosting grapefruit ships!

Laughter lingers, a tangerine tale,
Bright is the humor, light as a gale,
With citrus dreams that never fade,
Under dappled light, joy is made.

A Dance of Color Above

The sky puts on its best sunset dress,
Orange ribbons and a laugh, no less,
Clouds play hide and seek in their hue,
With shades so zany, it's a wild view.

We twirl like fruit in a blender,
Citrus giggles without a surrender,
Potato chips join in the parade,
Every crunch feels like a charade.

Balloons drift up like silly hopes,
Swirling patterns and tumbles with scopes,
As we chase tastes through the evening chill,
In this fruity ballet, we're king of the hill!

To the rhythm of joy, we lift our voice,
In this citrus realm, we rejoice,
The stars wink down with a cheeky show,
It's a dance of color with smiles aglow.

Last Light's Citrus Caress

As day gives way to twilight's hue,
A slice of sun bids us adieu,
We linger on rooftops, giggles abound,
In the zest of the moment, joy is found.

Sipping limeade, toes in the air,
With toast to laughter that lightens each care,
The sky reflects what our hearts have stored,
In the citrus glow, the spirit soared.

Witty comments flow, a citrus spree,
Every joke is a splash in our sea,
We relish the evening, the humor will chase,
As laughter lingers in this festooned space.

From dusk till dawn, pure mirth we'll proffer,
In this citrus embrace, we discover.
With every squeeze, this night feels blessed,
In last light's warm glow, we find our rest.

Lush Canopies of Warmth

Under the sun's squishy glow,
Lemons all giggle, putting on a show.
Bananas waltz with secret flair,
While oranges toss their peels in air.

Sipping on juice, we're stuck in bliss,
A citrus dance, what's not to miss?
Peachy dreams swirl, quite the delight,
In this fruity circus, everything's right.

Coconuts nod in sync, not shy,
Mangoes strut and wink an eye.
While grapey jokes roll through the air,
The zest for life, none could compare.

As the sun dips low, we all agree,
There's nothing quite like a fruity spree.
We laugh and feast, share every bite,
In warm embrace of a dazzling night.

Celestial Confections at Daybreak

Morning arrives in pastel hues,
Cookies sprinkled with sweet morning views.
Candy floss clouds float without care,
As marshmallow dreams fill the air.

The sun yawns wide, a pastry so bright,
Baking magic in the soft daylight.
Donald's breakfast, a crispy delight,
Fried egg winks—a comical sight.

Overhead, cupcakes swirl and twirl,
While doughnuts on strings begin to whirl.
A pancake parade marches so fine,
With syrup rivers, sweetened divine.

Giggles echo from heights above,
In the land of desserts, there's endless love.
At daybreak's call, we leap and play,
In a candy wonderland, we'll stay.

Slices of Summer in the Sky

A canvas painted in juicy shades,
Sunshine filters, creating lovely glades.
Watermelons float on clouds so high,
While popsicles stick, oh my, oh my!

Pineapples dance with tutus bright,
Salsa stomps under twinkling light.
Peaches giggle, they're never shy,
As jellybeans zoom and zip on by.

Cotton candy fluff makes quite a scene,
Sour patch kids cheer, oh how keen!
Lemonade fountains do a jig,
While lollipops join in, feeling big.

In this fruity fiesta, we all partake,
Beneath a rainbow, laughter we make.
Every slice is a burst of fun,
With sweetness shared under the sun.

The Day's Last Citrusy Breath

Evening whispers with a tangerine cheer,
Juicy oranges beckon us near.
In the twilight, flavors collide,
Lime-light jokes take us for a ride.

As night falls down with zesty embrace,
Bubbly drinks bubble up the place.
Chili macaroons giggle in delight,
As crunching snacks nibble through the night.

Limes and lemons in a friendly brawl,
Gather 'round, it's a fruity free-for-all!
Tangerine teasing, with peels in tow,
Jokes so silly, they sparkle and glow.

At day's end, we raise our spree,
To fruity mischief, wild and free.
With every bite, we take a stand,
In playful realms, hand in hand.

A Canvas of Evening's Flavors

Orange peels dance on the breeze,
Where twilight teases the leaves.
Lemonade smiles from a cloud,
As laughter bubbles, light and loud.

The sun wears a hat of spun gold,
While shadows tell tales, brave and bold.
A wink from a star, oh so sweet,
Makes the evening feel like a treat.

Bubbly chatter fills the air,
As critters prance without a care.
Juicy giggles twist and twirl,
In this surreal, whimsical whirl.

We toast to the flavors, bright and strange,
In this twilight magic, nothing's out of range.
With every bite, a chuckle bestowed,
As night wraps us in its playful load.

Sunset's Tangy Lattice

In a weave of pinks and bright yellows,
Witty clouds float like jolly fellows.
Each ray a jest, a sparkling jest,
As the day waves bye with a playful zest.

Chasing shadows, a game of peek,
The sun flicks its light, a cheeky sneak.
With hints of citrus in the air,
Nature's punchline, beyond compare.

Pineapple hats on rooftops wear,
While kites made of zest flap in the air.
Beneath this laughter, the world spins round,
In the riot of colors, joy is found.

As day fades to giggles, let's rejoice,
With our hearts as light as a gleeful voice.
To the quirky colors of the setting sun,
In this silly play, we're all having fun!

Citronade Clouds Unfurled

Fluffy clouds with a twist of twist,
Whisk through skies like a citrus mist.
Jokes pop like bubbles, bright and loud,
In the sweetness of sunset, we're all proud.

The horizon glows like candy floss,
As the sun gives a wink, what a boss!
Raspberry ribbons in the evening hue,
Crafting giggles, a zesty brew.

Sipping on giggles, a fizzy delight,
As the day dissolves into the night.
Each sunbeam tickling a verdant green,
This blend of hilarity, fit for a queen.

With laughter mixed in the final glow,
We frolic in jingles, bask in the show.
For in each sunset's burst of cheer,
Lies the joy of the day, oh so dear.

Hues that Speak of Day's End

The palette shifts to laugh and play,
Where silliness twirls at close of day.
Droplets of joy spill from the sun,
As night creeps in, the fun's just begun.

Crayon colors spill across the sky,
Each shade a wink, each hue a sigh.
Minty greens and peachy pinks,
In this carnival, the daylight blinks.

The moon joins in with a grin so wide,
As stars blush with their golden pride.
A comic show on the twilight stage,
Where fun ignites like a playful rage.

With shimmer and sparkle, the night is bold,
Crafting tales that never grow old.
In this tapestry of laughter and light,
We dance like kid clowns into the night.

Elysian Trails of Citrus Light

In a land where the lemons sing,
And oranges dance on a string,
Bananas giggle, try to hide,
While limes roll down the green slide.

A tangerine in a top hat,
Chasing after a savvy cat,
They prance beneath the giggly sun,
In this place, life is all in fun!

Grapes sip tea, discussing dreams,
While cherries laugh at silly schemes,
The clouds above are pink and bright,
Casting shadows of pure delight.

Peaches rise to play a tune,
Banana boats sail 'neath the moon,
With every beam, a joke they'll share,
In this citrus world without a care.

Sunset's Juicy Palette

The sun spills juice across the sea,
A splash of colors, wild and free,
The oranges wink at passing boats,
As laughter bubbles in tangy notes.

Plum pirates on their fruity quest,
Stealing slices, they think it's best,
With grapefruit guards on orange ships,
They giggle as the juice drips.

Beneath a sky of berry blush,
The fruits all gather, creating a hush,
For a joke that tickles every heart,
As juicy puns make the day start.

Watermelon dreams float by so sweet,
Where kiwi smiles and dancing feet,
Combine to make a fruity cheer,
In this palette, joy is near.

Colors That Taste of Bliss

A swirl of hues, a fruity dream,
Where laughter flows like a sweet cream,
The berries giggle, the apples leap,
In this orchard, secrets keep.

Tangerines in tutus twirl,
While lemon fairies skip and whirl,
Chasing joy on each vibrant hue,
As colors taste like a zesty brew!

Watering cans spill fizzy glee,
Squeezing smiles from every tree,
The sun sets low, a citrus kiss,
In a world of flavors filled with bliss.

Limes perform their stand-up show,
With citrus jokes that steal the glow,
And every laugh, a fragrance sweet,
In colors where the fun's complete.

Daydreams in Fruity Skies

Cotton candy clouds drift by,
Peachy whispers in the sky,
Pineapple dreams float like a kite,
In this world, everything feels bright.

Bubbling laughter from the trees,
Lemonade breezes with such ease,
Coconuts take a stroll in shade,
With every step, a juice parade.

Under this canopy of light,
Fruitful figures gleefully fight,
For the best joke of the day,
In this circus, who'd dare to play?

Watermelons juggle with flair,
As juicy antics fill the air,
Each blush and chuckle, pure delight,
In daydreams where fruits take flight.

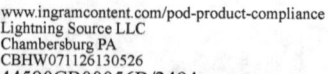